What Happens *After You Heal?*

Moving From Survival Into A Life That Is Fully Yours

Marie McKenzie, BSN, RN, MBA,
TRAUMA-INFORMED EDUCATOR

MARIE L MCKENZIE LLC

ISBN: 978-1-7371023-3-5 – eBook
ISBN: 979-8-9884482-5-9 - Paperback

For permissions, workshops, or bulk purchases, please contact:
Marie L McKenzie LLC at marielmckenzie@gmail.com
This book is a work of empowerment, healing, and encouragement. While it is designed to support survivors, it does not replace professional medical, psychological, or legal advice. The author and publisher disclaim any liability arising directly or indirectly from the use of the material contained in this book.

Disclaimer:
This book is for informational and inspirational purposes only. Some content may be inspired by widely accepted therapeutic practices, public resources, and general knowledge around trauma, healing, and mental health. However, the words, stories, and structure are original and drawn from personal insight, lived experience, and intentional encouragement. This book is not a substitute for professional therapy or legal counsel. Please seek help from licensed professionals as needed.

Trauma-Informed. Survivor-Centered. Always.

A note on language: This book uses trauma-informed, person-centered language throughout. The word "survivor" is used to honor agency and resilience. If any term does not feel right for your own experience, you are always welcome to substitute language that resonates best for you.

Table of Contents

Also by Marie McKenzie

Who Says You Can't Heal?

What Every Provider Should Know

From Stuck to Limitless

Things That Keep Me Up At Night

1000 Affirmations for Survivors

Available wherever books are sold online.

Dedication

For every survivor who did the hard work—
and then stood in the quiet, wondering what comes next.
For the ones who kept going
when keeping going was all they had.
May you find, in these pages,
permission to do more than survive.
You were made for more than this.
And this book is for the moment
you are brave enough to believe it.

Acknowledgments

To the survivors — you are the reason this book exists.

Your strength is not something I observed from a distance. I have sat with you in the hardest moments of your lives. I have watched you do things most people will never be asked to do. And I have had the privilege of witnessing what happens when someone decides — against everything — to keep going.

Your stories are the heartbeat of this work. Every chapter was written with you in mind.

To the healthcare professionals who show up every day with compassion and courage — I see you. The work you do in the quiet moments, in the difficult conversations, in the spaces where no one is watching — it matters more than you know. Keep going.

To my George — my steady, my safe place, my home. Your love makes this mission possible. Thank you for every moment of patience, every word of encouragement, and every time you reminded me why this work matters. I could not do this without you.

To my family and friends — thank you for your prayers, your presence, and your unwavering belief in what I am building. You carried me through the long hours and the hard days. Purpose is nurtured through community and love, and I have been blessed with both in abundance.

To my editors and beta readers — thank you for your sharp eyes, your honest feedback, and your commitment to excellence. You made this work stronger, clearer, and more impactful than I could have made it alone.

And to every survivor who chose healing — and then chose to share their story so others would not have to walk alone — this book is for you. What you survived took courage. What you continue to do takes more.

Thank you. All of you.

Note from Marie

I've sat with survivors at every stage of the journey — in emergency rooms, in courtrooms, in quiet spaces where they finally felt safe enough to speak. I've watched people come in broken and leave with the first fragile seeds of something new beginning to grow.

Those same places have held me as well—because my work isn't just professional. It's personal. I am a nurse, an educator, an advocate, and a survivor.

From both sides of that experience, I can tell you this: the world is rich in resources for the early stages of the healing journey, but painfully quiet about what comes after.

But there is a question that nobody seemed to be asking out loud — a question I've heard over and over, in the pauses during discussions, in the messages survivors sent me after they've completed formal work with therapists and others:

I think I'm healed. So why doesn't it feel like enough? What am I supposed to do now?

You've carried the weight of the beginning. You've done the hardest work a person can do. Now the question becomes: what comes after survival?

This book is my answer.

It's about moving forward with intention and clarity—not returning to the pain, but learning how to live beyond it.

You're a whole person, with dreams, desires, and a future still unfolding. You've survived the storm. Now let's talk about what it means to build a life on the other side.

With you, always —**Marie McKenzie, RN**

Introduction: After Healing, Then What?

Nobody tells you about the quiet that comes *after*.

After the crisis stage has passed. After the therapy sessions that once felt urgent begin to thin out. After you wake up one morning and realize, probably with a start, that you are not dreading the day.

That quiet should feel like relief. And in many ways, it does.

But it also brings a question that can catch you completely off guard — one that few people talk about openly, because everyone assumes healing is the finish line:

What happens after healing?

If you are holding this book, there is a good chance you have already walked through a significant portion of the healing journey. You have done difficult, courageous work. You have learned to cope, to process, to breathe through things that once knocked the wind out of you.

And now something has shifted.

You are no longer just trying to get through each day. You are beginning — cautiously, tentatively, sometimes with a sense of disbelief — to live again.

That is the moment this book was written for.

What This Book Is About

This is not a book about trauma. It is a book about what comes after — about the quiet, powerful, often-overlooked transition from healing to thriving.

We'll explore who you are now that you are no longer defined solely by survival. We'll talk about the strange discomfort of allowing joy back in, and why that discomfort does not mean something is wrong with you. We'll look at how relationships change, how trust returns, and how purpose begins to emerge from even the most painful chapters.

Most of all, this book is about a truth I have seen again and again, in the survivors I've met and spoken with and in my own life:

Healing is not the final chapter of your story. It is the doorway into the next one.

You do not need to rush. You do not need to have all the answers. You only need to be willing to take the next step.

Let's begin.

Chapter One: The Day You Stop Just Getting Through

There comes a moment — often quiet, often unexpected — when you realize that survival is no longer your full-time job.

For a long time, getting through the day was the goal. You learned to cope. You developed strategies. You showed up when you could and survived the days you couldn't. You rebuilt enough structure around yourself that life began to feel, if not easy, at least manageable.

And then, almost without noticing it, something changes.

The trauma no longer occupies every waking thought. The intensity of the triggers has softened. You catch yourself making plans for next month, or laughing at something without immediately feeling guilty about it, or realizing that you slept through the night without dreaming about what happened.

Progress. Real, meaningful progress.

And yet.

Something feels unfamiliar. Maybe even unsettling.

Because when survival is no longer the center of your life, a new question emerges that nobody warned you about:

Now what?

The Move from Surviving to Living

Survival is not weakness. It is strength in its most raw and necessary form. But survival was never meant to be permanent.

In the early stages after trauma, you do what you have to do. You manage emotions as best you can. You find ways to function even on the days when functioning feels impossible. You get through.

But at some point — slowly, and often gradually you don't recognize it at first — survival begins to give way to something else. You start to notice moments when you are not just enduring life, but actually engaging with it. You make a plan for the future. You feel a flicker of possibility.

These moments may be brief. You might question them: Is this real? Am I actually okay? What if this doesn't last?

Those questions are natural. Growth often feels uncertain before it feels secure. But these moments are not accidents. They are evidence that something within you has changed. You are moving — step by careful step — from surviving to living.

When Healing Feels "Finished"

Many survivors reach a point where they begin to wonder: Is healing complete? The acute pain has lessened. The weight is no longer constant. Life feels more navigable than it has in years.

And yet there are still moments — a memory that surfaces unexpectedly, an emotional echo from out of nowhere, a quiet ache on an anniversary — that remind you the past has not disappeared entirely.

This can lead to confusion. If I am healed, why do I still feel this sometimes?

Here is what I want you to understand:

Healing is not the absence of all difficult emotions. It is the ability to experience life fully — without being controlled by what happened.

You may still remember. You may still feel. But those moments no longer define your entire existence. That is what healing looks like. Not the erasure of the past — but the restoration of your ability to live fully in the present.

Letting Go of Healing as an Identity

For some survivors, healing itself becomes part of who they are. After spending so much time focused on recovery, it becomes a central thread in how they see themselves. I am someone who is healing. I am working through trauma.

There is nothing wrong with that identity — it served you, and it honors the real work you have done. But there comes a time when that identity begins to feel like a room you have outgrown.

You are still a survivor. That will always be true. But you are also so much more than that. You are a person with dreams, desires, talents, and purpose — qualities that exist beyond what you have experienced. Letting go of healing as your primary identity does not mean forgetting your journey. It means allowing yourself to grow beyond it.

You Are Allowed to Live Fully

Perhaps the most important truth in this entire book is this: You are allowed to live a full life. You are allowed to experience joy. You are allowed to pursue goals, build relationships, take risks, and embrace new opportunities — without having to earn any of them or feel guilty.

Living fully is not a betrayal of what you have been through. It is the greatest possible testament to your resilience.

* * *

A Moment to Reflect

Take a moment to sit with these questions. There are no right or wrong answers — only honest ones.

- Are you still focused primarily on healing, or are you beginning to notice a shift toward living?
- What feels different for you now compared to where you started this journey?
- What would it mean to you to stop defining yourself primarily by your healing?

Healing brought you this far. Now it is time to begin building what comes next — not just a life that is manageable, but a life that feels meaningful, whole, and fully your own.

Chapter Two: Who Am I Now?

Healing brings relief.

But it also brings a question many survivors are completely unprepared for — a question that arrives not in the middle of the hardest days, but in the quiet that follows them:

If trauma is no longer defining every part of my life... who am I?

For a long time, trauma shaped how you saw yourself. It influenced your decisions, your relationships, and the way you protected your heart. During healing, much of your energy went toward understanding what happened and learning how to live with it. That work is sacred. It took real courage.

But as that season begins to lift, something unexpected happens. The fear that once filled every corner of your day starts to release its grip. The vigilance that once felt necessary begins to soften. And in that new quiet space appears — an opening where survival once lived and healing once demanded everything you had.

And in that stillness, a quiet voice asks: Who am I now?

When Identity Was Built Around Surviving

Many survivors find that trauma becomes intertwined with identity in ways that aren't always obvious in the beginning. You may have come to see yourself as the one who endured—the one who survived something difficult. The one who had to be strong when everything felt unsafe.

It makes sense. Those identities helped you survive. They gave meaning to experiences that might otherwise have felt impossible to hold.

But healing creates the opportunity to expand beyond those roles and open a door you may not even have known was there.

You Are More Than What Happened to You

You are not only a person who overcame trauma. There are pieces of you that didn't vanish—they simply went quiet while you focused on staying alive. They are still there, waiting for you to come back to them.

Sometimes survivors notice that returning to themselves feels unfamiliar or even frightening. The things you once brought joy may feel distant, and you may not know where to begin. Perhaps you once loved to write, or to dance, or to lose yourself in learning something new. Healing allows you to give yourself permission to explore what still feels true and alive with who you are now.

The Permission to Rediscover Yourself

This stage of healing often brings a complicated mix of enthusiasm and hesitation. Some survivors experience genuine guilt when life begins to feel better: Is it okay for me to be happy again? Am I leaving my past behind if I move forward?

The answer: moving forward does not erase the past. Your story will always include what you have lived through. But it can also include growth, joy, connection, and purpose. Your life is not limited to one chapter.

You are not starting over. You are continuing — with more awareness, more strength, and more of yourself than before.

Identity Expands — It Does Not Get Replaced

Rediscovering yourself is not about becoming someone entirely new or reinventing your identity. It's about reconnecting with the parts of you that have always been there — and allowing them to grow in ways they never had the chance to before.

Some pieces of you may feel familiar, like old friends finding their way back. Others may feel new: strengths shaped by what you've survived, compassion deepened by what you've known, and clarity born from what you've had to let go. Identity isn't a fixed point. It unfolds shifts, and expand. It's something you inhabit more fully as you learn to live in your own skin again.

* * *

A Moment to Reflect

These questions are not meant to be answered all at once. Return to them as many times as you need to.

• What are three qualities that describe who you are today — beyond your history with trauma?

• What interests or passions feel like they want to come back to life?

• What parts of your identity have grown stronger because of your healing journey?

You are not starting over. You are continuing— with more awareness, more strength, and more of yourself than you have reclaimed along the way.

Chapter Three: Your Story Is Bigger Than Your Trauma

Trauma has a way of demanding attention.

When something painful happens — especially something that reshapes your sense of safety, trust, and identity — it is natural for that experience to become the lens through which you see everything else. For a time, that focus is not only understandable; it's necessary.

But eventually, something changes. The trauma story begins to settle and shift into its rightful place. And when it does, something important becomes visible that wasn't before:

The trauma chapter is real. But it was never the whole story.

When One Chapter Feels Like the Whole Book

Many survivors spend years revisiting what happened — in therapy, in support groups, in quiet conversations with trusted people. This work matters. It brings clarity, creates validation, and gives shape to something that once felt impossible to hold.

But at some point, something else starts to happen. You notice that you no longer need to revisit every detail. The memories still exist, but they no longer dominate every thought about your future. The story is still yours—it just isn't the only one anymore.

Letting the Story Find Its Proper Place

Letting trauma take its proper place does not mean ignoring what happened. Your wounds were real. Your resilience is real. Both deserve to be honored.

What it means is this: your life contains more than that one period. Your story also includes the people who have loved you, the goals you are working toward, the lessons that changed you, and the moments of peace and connection that continue to unfold. Those parts of your story deserve space too.

Growth Does Not Erase Truth

Some survivors worry that moving forward means minimizing what they went through. The answer is no. Growth does not erase truth of what happened. *It expands it.* Your story becomes larger, not smaller. The trauma remains real, but it no longer overshadows everything else that is also true about you.

Think of it this way: a single powerful chapter does not diminish the chapters that follow. It deepens them. The reader carries what they learned from that chapter into everything that comes next. Your story works the same way.

Making Space for New Chapters

When trauma takes its proper place, something beautiful becomes possible—new chapters. You start pursuing interests that bring meaning and joy. You invest in relationships that feel safe. You imagine goals that once felt completely out of reach.

These new experiences don't replace the past. They expand your life beyond it — living proof that your story is still unfolding.

* * *

A Moment to Reflect

Your story is not finished. These questions are an invitation to see how much of it remains to be written.

- What parts of your life exist outside of the trauma story? What experiences, relationships, or qualities make up those other chapters?
- What new chapters feel like they are beginning to open for you now?
- If a trusted friend were describing the full you — not just the healing-focused you — what would they say?

The trauma chapter is part of your story. But it is not the whole story. And it never has to be.

Chapter Four: Learning to Feel Safe Again

One of the deepest wounds trauma leaves behind is not a memory. It is not a scar. It is the loss of something most people take entirely for granted:

Trust.

Trust in people. Trust in institutions. Trust in the idea that safety is even possible. And sometimes — most painfully — trust in your own judgment and instincts.

For many survivors, that trust wasn't worn down slowly. It was shattered in a single moment. And in response, your mind and body did exactly what they were designed to do: they learned. Be careful. Stay alert. Protect yourself.

These responses are not signs that you are broken or flawed. They are evidence that you are human — and that your system worked doing what it needed to protect you.

Why Trust Feels So Difficult to Rebuild

In the early stages of healing, these protective instincts make complete sense. You may have become more selective about who you allow close. You may scan for hidden intentions, or pull back when relationships feels overwhelming.

These patterns served you. They kept you safe during a time when you were most vulnerable. But as healing deepens, a new question arises: *Will I always feel this guarded? Is it still possible to truly trust someone again?*

The answer is yes. But trust doesn't return in the way it left. It comes back differently — slower, steadier, and more discerning.

Trust Grows Through Experience, Not Decisions

Trust isn't something you choose. It's something that grows when you create the conditions in which it is possible.

Trust returns slowly, through safe and consistent experiences—a friend who listens without judgment, a colleague who shows the same respect day after day, or a partner who keeps their word. These moments may seem small, but they are not. They're teaching your nervous system something it needed to learn: not every person is unsafe.

Rebuilding Without Abandoning Your Wisdom

Rebuilding trust is about building something more intentional than what existed before trauma. You are allowed to protect yourself. You are also allowed to experience meaningful connection. Both can be true at once.

Healthy trust grows through people who show up consistently, who honor your pace, who respect your boundaries without being asked twice. Trust is not forced. It develops naturally when true safety is present.

The Most Important Trust: The One with Yourself

Of all the forms of trust trauma can damage, self-trust may be the most devastating. You may have spent years second-guessing your instincts, wondering whether your sense of people and situations could be trusted.

Here is the truth that healing reveals: the responsibility for harm belongs to the person who caused it — not you. Your instincts did not fail you. The people and systems that were supposed to protect you failed you.

As that reality settles in, you begin reconnecting with your intuition. You become more able to notice what feels safe and what does not. And start trusting your own voice again.

When you trust yourself, relationships begin to feel less like a gamble and more like a choice.

---

* * *

A Moment to Reflect

Trust is not rebuilt in a single conversation or decision. These questions can help you trace where it already lives.

- What experiences — however small — have helped you begin to rebuild trust with others?
- What qualities make someone feel safe to you?
- In what ways are you learning to trust your own instincts and judgment again?

Trust was broken. But it can be rebuilt — not by rushing the process, but by allowing safety, one consistent moment at a time, to show you that connection is still possible.

Chapter Five: Relationships After Trauma

Healing does not happen in isolation — but it does influence the way you experience every relationship in your life.

For some survivors, trauma created distance. Emotional walls that formed during the most vulnerable moments may still be standing, even as the crisis has passed. For others, trauma created a painful paradox: a deep longing for connection, paired with a deep reluctance to trust it.

Both responses are normal. Both make complete sense. And both can change.

What Your Body Carries

After trauma, the nervous system becomes highly attuned to potential danger. Even when you consciously know you are safe, your body may still react to certain cues — a shift in tone, an unexpected touch — with a speed and intensity that can feel out of proportion for the moment.

This is not you being irrational. This is your body doing its job. The same system that protected you is still running its protective protocols. Knowing this changes things. The goal is not to eliminate protective responses, but to gradually help your nervous system learn that safety is available now.

Boundaries Are Not Walls

One of the most transformative turn healing brings is a new relationship with boundaries. Many people — especially those who experienced trauma early in life — were never taught that they were allowed to have them.

Healing changes that in a profound way. You begin to understand that you have the right to decide what feels safe and respectful. Boundaries are not rejection — they are honest communication about what you need in order to show up fully for yourself.

A boundary can sound like: I'm not comfortable talking about that right now. I need some time before I respond. And healthy people, people worth having in your life, will hear those statements and respond with love and respect.

What Safe People Actually Look Like

Safe people are not perfect. But they are consistent. They listen without judgment, respect your boundaries the first time, honor your pace, communicate honestly, and show up again and again in a pattern your nervous system can learn to recognize.

Consistency is everything. When someone treats you with kindness and respect repeatedly, your nervous system loosens its grip, and your body starts to relax. Your guard begins to lower — not because you decided to lower it, but because you have been given enough evidence to feel safe doing so.

When Relationships No Longer Fit

Healing brings clarity — and sometimes that clarity is uncomfortable. As you grow, you may recognize that some relationships no longer feel healthy. Some people may struggle to respect your boundaries. Some may not be able to meet you at the level of honesty that healing has made non-negotiable for you.

Letting go of a relationship is not easy. But sometimes it is necessary — not as punishment or in anger, but as an act of self-respect and protection for the person you are becoming.

You are allowed to build relationships that feel safe. You are allowed to be seen and understood without fear.

* * *

A Moment to Reflect

Healthy relationships are one of the most powerful environments for continued healing. These questions can help you assess where you are.

- Who in your life feels emotionally safe and consistently supportive?
- What boundaries help you feel respected and present in your relationships?
- What qualities do you most want in the relationships you are building going forward?

You deserve relationships that bring peace, support, and genuine encouragement into your life. And you are allowed to create them.

Chapter Six: The Courage to Experience Joy

For many survivors, healing is not the hardest part.

Allowing joy back into their lives is.

That might sound surprising. After everything a survivor goes through, most people would assume happiness would be welcomed without hesitation. But the reality is often far more complex.

Why Joy Can Feel Dangerous

After trauma, the nervous system learns to treat vigilance as safety, and treat it like a standing order Your mind learns to scan for danger. Your body learns to stay prepared. Over time, survival mode becomes the default setting — and even when life becomes calmer, your system may still be running the old program.

And because of that, joy can feel like foreign territory. Distant. Like something that belongs to other people but not to you.

I remember a time in my own life when things began to feel lighter, and instead of relief, I felt uneasy. I was determined not to let happiness back in and kept waiting for something to go wrong. It took time to understand that what I was feeling wasn't a warning sign — it was something I had been lost touch with. The absence of crisis felt strange because crisis had become a the normal I recognized.

The Fear That Shadows Joy

When good things begin to happen, a quiet internal voice can appear: Don't get too comfortable. Something bad might happen. This won't last.

These thoughts are not signs that something is wrong with you. They are echoes of the past. Your mind is trying to protect you from disappointment. But healing introduces a new possibility: you can experience joy without abandoning awareness. You can embrace both.

Joy Does Not Betray Your Past

One of the most persistent barriers to joy is guilt. Survivors wonder: Is it okay for me to feel happy, given what happened?

Joy is not a betrayal of your past. It is evidence that healing is working.

Joy does not wipe away what happened. Joy honors your survival. Allowing happiness into your life is not forgetting — it is claiming the future you earned through all that hard, painful, courageous work.

Joy Returns in Small Moments First

Joy rarely returns all at once. It comes back slowly, quietly — in ordinary moments you might almost miss. A real laugh during a conversation. The feeling of your body relaxing during a walk. A few hours of genuine absorption in something that interests you.

These moments are your nervous system learning, one experience at a time, that safety is available. That good things can happen. That happiness does not have to end in pain.

Giving Yourself Permission

Joy often begins with a deliberate act of permission. Permission to feel peace without interrogating it. Permission to experience happiness without guilt. Permission to enjoy your life without waiting for something to go wrong.

You do not have to earn joy. Every moment you allow it; you reinforce a new truth: your story did not end with trauma. It is still unfolding — with resilience, with growth, and with the return of something that was interrupted, but not forgotten.

* * *

A Moment to Reflect

Joy may be closer than it feels. These questions are an invitation to look for where it already lives.

- What moments bring you a genuine sense of peace or happiness, even briefly?
- Where do you notice yourself holding back from enjoyment? What are you afraid will happen if you let joy in?
- What would it look like to give yourself more permission to experience joy without conditions?

Joy is not something you have to chase. It is something you are allowed to receive. And every time you welcome it, you take another step into the life that is waiting for you.

Chapter Seven: Finding Your Voice Again

As healing deepens, many survivors begin to reclaim something they did not always realize they had lost:

Their voice.

How Trauma Silences

Sometimes the silence is literal — you felt unable to speak about what happened for months or years. Fear of not being believed, fear of judgment, fear of reliving the experience made silence feel safer.

But often the silence is more subtle. You may have stopped expressing opinions that might cause conflict. You may have learned to minimize your own needs to keep peace. You discovered that staying small felt safer than being seen — and so you became very good at staying small.

Over time, these patterns settle into an inner narrative about yourself— that your voice doesn't matter. Healing begins to dismantle that belief — slowly, sometimes painfully, with a great deal of practice.

What Reclaiming Your Voice Actually Looks Like

For some survivors, reclaiming voice includes advocacy or public speaking. For most, it happens in much quieter, more intimate moments. It sounds like: I'm not comfortable with that. I need more time to think. No.

These words may seem simple. For someone who has spent years silencing themselves in order to survive, they are acts of extraordinary courage.

You Are Allowed to Participate in Your Own Life

Reclaiming your voice means remembering something foundational: you have the right to take up space in your own life.

Not a supporting character. Not as someone who moves around other people's needs. You are the protagonist — the one whose experience, needs, and truth matter.

You're allowed to name what you feel, to have preferences, set limits, and disagree. You're permitted to protect your time, energy, and emotional well-being. This is not being selfishness. This what reclaiming your life looks like.

Trusting Your Inner Voice

Reclaiming your voice is not only about what you say to others. It is about learning to listen to — and trust — the voice within yourself.

Trauma can cause deep disconnection from your own instincts. Healing gradually restores that connection. Your intuition was not broken by trauma. It was drowned out. As the noise of survival quiets, you begin to hear it again.

Your voice carries something powerful: the truth of who you are. And the world is better when it can hear you.

---

* * *

A Moment to Reflect

Your voice strengthens with every use. These questions are an invitation to notice where it already speaks.

- In what ways have you begun expressing yourself more clearly or honestly than you used to?
- Where do you still find yourself going quiet when you could speak up?
- What would it look like to honor your voice more fully — in one specific area of your life, starting this week?

Your voice matters — even when it shakes. Especially then. Because it carries something the world needs: the truth of who you are.

Chapter Eight: Purpose After Pain

There is a question many survivors eventually ask once healing has started to make sense — usually not in a single dramatic moment, but in a slow, growing awareness that creeps up somewhere between the ordinary moments of your day.

What do I do with everything I have lived through?

First, Let's Say This Clearly

Trauma is not a gift. It is not a blessing in disguise. It is not something that happened to you in order to make you stronger. You did not need to go through what you went through in order for your life to have meaning.

What is true — and what healing gradually reveals — is this: while you cannot change what happened, you can choose what you do with what you have learned. That is where purpose begins.

Purpose Does Not Have to Be Loud

There is sometimes an unspoken assumption that purpose after pain needs to look dramatic — that it means starting a movement, writing a book, becoming a public advocate. And, for some people, those paths are the right ones.

But purpose is not required to be loud or visible. For many survivors, it shows up in the quiet, consistent work of being present for other people in ways that only someone who has known real pain can manage.

The Gifts You Carry Without Knowing It

After doing the hard work of healing, survivors carry gifts they often don't fully recognize. A particular quality of listening. The ability to be present with someone in pain without trying to rush them through it. A capacity for empathy grounded in lived experience. An instinct for when someone needs to be heard versus challenged. These are not small things. They are extraordinary things.

Your Story Expands Beyond the Pain

There comes a point in healing when your story refuses to be defined by the old narrative. It is no longer only about what happened to you. It is also about who you have become, what you have learned, and how you continue to grow.

That turning point is one of the most powerful transformations healing makes possible. It moves you from being defined by your wound to being shaped by your wisdom. Purpose does not require a plan. It unfolds through following what feels meaningful and noticing what ignites something inside you.

* * *

A Moment to Reflect

Purpose often reveals itself quietly. These questions can help you notice where it is already showing up.

- What strengths have you developed through your healing journey that show up in your everyday life?
- When do you feel most like you are contributing something meaningful?
- If your pain could be turned into something helpful, what might that look like? No pressure in this question — only curiosity.

Your story did not end with what you went through. It expanded. And within that expansion, there is space for meaning, impact, and a life that continues to grow.

Chapter Nine: Building a Life That Feels Like Yours

One of the most meaningful realizations that comes after healing is also one of the simplest:

You get to choose what comes next.

That might not sound like a revelation. But for someone who spent significant time in survival mode — where decisions were shaped by fear, by the need to protect yourself, by the relentless demands of just getting through — it is a profound shift.

When Choice Feels Unfamiliar

The realization that you have agency over your future can feel both exhilarating and disorienting. Questions you may not have dared ask yourself for years begin to surface: What kind of life do I actually want to build? What environments make me feel like the best version of myself? What truly matters to me?

These are not small questions. They are the questions that begin to shape everything that follows.

Getting Clear on Your Values

Building a life that feels genuinely yours begins with understanding what you actually value — not what you were told to value, not what seemed safest, but what matters to you at the deepest and most honest level.

Trauma creates significant distance from our values; so much energy goes into survival that there is barely room to consider what matters at all. Healing creates the space to ask that question again. When your daily life begins to align with those values, you begin to feel more grounded—more like yourself.

Reconnecting with What Brings Life

Part of building your life is reconnecting with what brings you alive — the activities, experiences, and ways of being that make you feel like the fullest version of yourself. This might mean returning to something you loved before trauma reshaped your life, or exploring something entirely new.

These steps toward what awakens you are not distractions from the real work. They are the real work. They are how you learn, through experience rather than theory, that your life can hold good things.

Allowing Yourself to Set Goals Again

Trauma can quietly erode your relationship with hope. When life has been unpredictable or painful, it can feel safer not to want too much. Healing gives you the capacity to imagine something beyond survival.

You are allowed to want things again. Goals don't have to be grand. They can begin with simple intentions: improving your health, deepening one relationship, learning something new, or contributing to something meaningful. Each step reinforces a truth that trauma tried to take from you: your future is not determined by your past.

You are not rebuilding your life from nothing. You are building it from strength — and this time, it gets to feel like yours.

---

* * *

A Moment to Reflect

You are the author of what comes next. These questions are an invitation to begin writing.

• What values feel most important to you right now, as you think about the life you want to build?

- What environments, relationships, or experiences make you feel most alive and most like yourself?
- What is one small, concrete step you can take this week toward a life that reflects what you actually value?

You are not rebuilding your life from nothing. You are building it from strength. And this time — it gets to feel like yours.

Chapter Ten: The Life You Deserve

There is a truth many survivors struggle to accept — even after years of healing, even after doing all the work, even after everything that is written in this book:

You deserve a rich and meaningful life.

You might read that sentence and agree. *I know that.* On the surface, it makes sense. But there is a significant difference between knowing something in your mind and believing it in the places where grief rises up — in the quiet hours, in the moments when old messages resurface, in the choices you make about what you allow or don't allow or deny yourself to hope for. Belief takes time to rebuild. Healing is creating enough safety inside yourself for it to slowly simmer and settle.

The Messages Trauma Leaves Behind

Long after the experience itself has passed, the messages it left behind can linger. They surface in the quiet moments—in doubt, in hesitation, in the instinct to shrink yourself or expect less.

Even when you understand that what happened was not your fault, those emotional imprints can remain. They are not evidence of weakness or inadequate healing, but of how deeply you were shaped by what happened, and how much courage it takes to live beyond those old narratives. And they respond to patience, compassion, and the slow accumulation of new experiences that tell a different story.

Your Worth Was Never Taken

What happened to you does not determine your worth. Your value was never conditional on the actions of others or the circumstances you survived. You deserved safety. You deserved respect. You deserved protection. If those things were not given to you, that was a failure of the people and systems that should have protected you — not a reflection of your value.

Learning to Believe, Not Just Understand

Much of this deeper work is about closing the gap between understanding and believing. You may understand every word in this chapter. The real transformation happens when that understanding begins to settle into lived experience — when you catch yourself wanting something and don't immediately feel guilty, or when you allow joy without waiting for it to be taken away.

Changing the way you speak to yourself is part of this process. It means shifting from the critical inner voice that fixates on your fears and insecurities to one that recognizes your strength and treats you with the same compassion you would extend to someone you love.

You Are Allowed to Want More

As you begin to embrace this shift change, something different opens up. You start to allow yourself to want more — more peace, more connection, more fulfillment, more of the specific things that make your life feel like yourself.

Wanting more for your life is not unrealistic. It is not arrogant. It is human. A full life after trauma does not mean pretending the past didn't happen. It means allowing new experiences to take their place beside them.

You are allowed to have a good life. Not someday. Not after proving something. Now.

---

* * *

A Moment to Reflect

You deserve to be asked what you want. These questions are an invitation to begin answering honestly.

- What does a fulfilling life look like to you today — not someday, but now, at this specific point in your journey?
- What experiences or relationships already bring genuine meaning into your life?
- In what one area could you practice treating yourself with the same compassion you would extend to someone you love?

You were never meant only to survive. You were meant to live. And that life — your life — is still waiting for you.

Chapter Eleven: When the Past Shows Up Uninvited

Even deep into your healing journey — even in a life that feels different and better — there will be moments when the past shows up without warning.

A smell. A sound. A phrase someone uses that shouldn't mean anything. And suddenly, without your permission, you are somewhere else—right back to the moment you thought you'd left behind.

When this happens, the thoughts that often follow are some of the most defeating in the entire healing process: Why is this happening again? Am I going backward? Is this ever going to get better?

This Is Not a Setback

When the past shows up like this, it's easy to assume something is wrong. But these moments are not proof that you've failed or slipped backward. They're reminders that you're human and that healing doesn't follow a straight line.

Healing doesn't erase the past; it changes how you live with it. The goal was never to wipe out every memory. The goal isn't to make every memory disappear. It's to be able to remember without being overwhelmed by it—to have a memory without being undone by it.

What Is Actually Different Now

Before healing, a triggered memory could pull you completely out of the present. It might have hijacked your thoughts for hours. Something is different now. You can notice what is happening. You can pause. You can recognize, even in the middle of it, this is a memory. I'm not there anymore. I'm here and I'm safe.

That recognition — the capacity to observe the memory instead of being consumed by it — is a real marker of healing. It may not feel dramatic, but it represents meaningful change.

Responding with Compassion Rather Than Frustration

When an old memory hits without warning, it can shake you. But, your response matters as much as the experience itself. Instead of fighting the memory or shaming yourself for having it, you can acknowledge it for what it is: a piece of your history. Not your present. You're here now and you're safe.

That switch from self-criticism to self-compassion is the most powerful choices available to you.

Simple Practices for Coming Back to the Present

Grounding practices help return you to the present when the past pulls you away. These do not have to be complicated. Slow, deliberate breathing. Looking around and naming what you see. Noticing the sensations under your feet or in your hands. Reminding yourself: I'm here. I'm safe.

These small practices have helped me and many others. Over time, moments like these becomes less frequent, less intense, and easier to move through. Your life grows larger, and the past begins to take its proper place within that larger picture.

* * *

A Moment to Reflect

How you respond when the past visits is one of the clearest measures of healing. These questions invite honest reflection.

- What helps you return to the present moment when the past shows up unexpectedly?
- What reminds you that you are safe in the present, even when old memories surface?

• How have your responses to these moments changed over the course of your healing journey?

The past may visit from time to time. But it no longer lives here. You do.

Chapter Twelve: You Are More Than What Happened to You

We have come a long way together.

From the strange quiet that follows healing, through identity and trust, relationships, joy, through voice, purpose, the life you are building, and through the uninvited visits of the past and back again to the present.

And now we arrive at perhaps the most important truth in this entire book.

When Survival Becomes Identity

After a life-altering experience, it is natural for that experience to shape how see yourself and the world. The word survivor represents something real and meaningful and courageous. There is nothing wrong with that.

But healing deepens the question. Is that the whole story?

Your Life Is a Mosaic

Imagine your life as a mosaic — a complex image made up of many different pieces. One piece represents what you endured. Another reflects the healing work you've done. But there are many other pieces: your relationships, your passions, your values, your creativity, your humor, your purpose, the distinct way you see the world.

When you step back and look at the whole picture, a different understanding emerges: the trauma is part of the image — an important part that shaped everything around it. But it is not the whole image. It never was.

Expanding, Not Erasing

Living beyond the survivor identity does not mean forgetting. It does not mean pretending anything was smaller than it was. You're not cutting that part of yourself off. You're letting it sit alongside everything else that's true about you.

You are still becoming. There are parts of you that had to be quiet just to make it through the day and are finally able to come forward now.

The Future Is No Longer Limited

When trauma sits too close to your identity, it quietly narrows what you believe is possible. It builds walls you don't always notice until you start healing. Healing dismantles those walls—sometimes not all at once, but slowly, with intention.

You begin to see a future that isn't confined by only what happened to you.

You are not defined by one chapter. You are shaped by all of them.

Final Words

I have had the privilege, over many years, of walking alongside survivors at different points of this journey. And again and again, I have witnessed a particular moment—one I look for, and never take for granted.

A moment I treasure.

The moment when someone realizes they are no longer defined by what happened to them.

It shows up differently every time. Sometimes it is a statement said with surprise: *I really feel okay*. Sometimes it is a goal pursued, or a boundary held, or a laugh that arrives without guilt or apology. Sometimes it is simply the way someone walks into a room now.

But it is always unmistakable. And it usually changes everything.

You have survived.

You have healed.

And now you are living.

Not as someone defined by trauma. Not as someone whose story ended with the hardest chapter. But as someone who is still becoming. Still growing. Still writing pages that have not yet been written.

Your story did not end with what happened to you. It did not end with healing. It continues — in the life you are building now, and in the life that is still ahead.

Affirmations for the Life Ahead

These affirmations are for the life you are building — carry them with you.

I am more than what happened to me.

I am allowed to take up space in my own life.

Healing brought me here. I choose what comes next.

I trust myself to know what feels safe.

I deserve relationships that bring me peace.

Joy is not a betrayal of my past. It is evidence of my healing.

My voice matters. Even when it shakes.

My pain has purpose. My story is not finished.

I am building a life that reflects who I am becoming.

I deserve a full and meaningful life — now, not someday.

The past no longer defines me. I am still becoming.

I am allowed to begin.

Continue the Journey

If these affirmations spoke to you, you may also enjoy:

1000 Affirmations for Survivors
A companion resource by Marie McKenzie

A powerful collection of healing-centered affirmations designed to encourage, ground, and empower you through every stage of recovery and rebuilding.

Available online.

An Invitation

As you close this book, take a moment. Not to look back at where you've been— but to look forward at where you're going.

What kind of life do you want to continue building?

Whatever your answer – no matter how tentative, uncertain, or underserving it may feel in this moment–know this:

You are allowed to begin.

About the Author

Marie McKenzie, BSN, RN, MBA, CEN is a Registered Nurse, Sexual Assault Nurse Examiner, Award-Winning & Bestselling author, and the Founder and CEO of the International Sexual Assault Coaching Institute (ISACI)

She has dedicated her life to bridging the gap between clinical excellence and compassionate recovery.

With over two decades of experience, Marie brings a unique perspective to her work; both professional expertise and lived wisdom. Her background as a clinician, advocate, and fellow survivor informs her specialized approach to trauma-informed care and healthcare professional education.

She is the author of several impactful works, including *Who Says You Can't Heal?: Overcoming and Thriving After Sexual Assault, What Every Provider Should Know: A trauma-Informed Guide for Healthcare Professionals, and Things That Keep Me Up At Night (memoir).*

Through ISACI, Marie offers comprehensive trauma-informed trainings, workshops, speaking engagements, and digital resources designed to empower both survivors and the providers who serve them.

Learn more about Marie and ISACI

Scan the QR code below

Trauma-Informed. Survivor-Centered. Always.

www.ingramcontent.com/pod-product-compliance
Lightning Source LLC
LaVergne TN
LVHW011053110826
845149LV00015B/3479

* 9 7 9 8 9 8 8 4 4 8 2 5 9 *